DEAR DIARY OF '21

Matthew Wu

BookLeaf Publishing

India | USA | UK

Presentation by *BookLeaf Publishing*

Web: www.bookleafpub.com

E-mail: info@bookleafpub.com

ISBN: 9789358362206

First edition 2021

1.   DEAR DIARY OF '21

Dear diary of '21,

It's May 13th and day one

of an exploration and indulgement

of your celebration and resentment

My eyes are glued down, onto the pavement

As I read out loud, to you my statement

I will remember this as the day when

I first said dear diary with fulfillment

I know not what these days will inspire

I can speak freely now, my desires

I can speak the truth here, my heart afire

Diary, between us, there is no liar

Sitting here beside the windows

As I write about my sorrows

A feeling inside as if it's hollow

A glimpse outside I'll need to borrow

I'm also here to share my joys

You're here so that you hear my voice

Telling you how I, went out with the boys

Feeling so high on life and overjoyed

Dear diary of '21,

I'm really hoping we'll have some fun

I'll tell you everything and how it runs

I know you'll be here when I need someone

.

2. WAITING

It's so easy to say I'll do it later

It's so easy to play now and say whatever

It's so easy to say no and blame willpower

But you got it in you, I know you'll power –

Through these times,

Writing down these lines,

Full of rhymes,

Wondering when the time

Will be right

For me to light

The flame up and get 'er going

3, 2, 1 go and and now we're floating

Keep it up so smoothly, the way we flowing

Fly it up so high that it's snowing

And you know we're showing-

Off to all those who said we're just posing

Too busy sniffing around, and nosing-

To notice us spacebound and gloating

Down at them like you don't know what you saying

I don't mean to brag, but I'm just saying

You'd have been much better off without the waiting

So pick yourself up and stop procrastinating

Stop worrying about how the past keeps on fading

And think about how the future just keeps on coming-

So quick it's here before you even know it

Yesterday you said today but you blew it

You still got time today, so go get it

I promise if you do, you won't regret it

Today you'll say tomorrow

So get it right now, don't let your day end in sorrow

3. TUG OF WAR

When people ask my how I've been doing

I just say the things they want to be hearing

Hold up, wait, I was just kidding

Nobody's really at that level of caring

I wanna stand out

But I don't wanna be different

I wanna fit in

But feels like something is missin'

I wanna be alone

But don't wanna be lonely

I like having some company

But hate when it's annoying

My life's a game of tug of war

And I'm the rope

That I, myself am tearing apart

And I'm looking for hope

But that's the hard part

Cause as soon as I spoke-

These words, I don't know where to start

Maybe I should just cut apart the rope

4. TIME

I really can't believe I'm in 11 already

I don't wanna leave, I don't think that I'm ready

I'd love it if I could stay how I am forever

But the world moves on, and I know you're-

Not really satisfied with where you are now-

Anyways so I really don't get how

You'd be happy like this either way

Cause right now, feels like it's every day

That you get up, but aren't really awake

In the blink of a heavy eyelid, you look back in dismay

That the minute hand made another revolution, insane

You thought resting a moment longer was the solution, but hey

That's just like life, right

It takes the blink of an eye,

A really long blink

To realize you've been asleep

And all that the time you think

Was on your side has begun to seep

Away and gone forever so quick

You didn't even realize how long it's been

Yet you're still feeling tired and sick

Of living the same day on repeat,

It's getting under your skin

Looking back at all you did in the past

Instead of planning for the future,

Trapped in the shadow it's cast

Still thinking about how you ain't sure

What you'll do when you're older.

Time, how it just flies by so fast

5. LIVING ON REPEAT

I know this might sound a little weird

But for the past while, I've been living on repeat

I know this was the outcome I had feared

Getting through this won't be an easy feat

Every day, the same stuff

Every day my life's rough

Every day that I can think of

I've had about enough

Thought I was on track to getting better

Thought that I'd found the key to being happy

But I was on track to a temporary shelter

And now I see the train coming at me

It's about time I got out of this place

On the surface all well and good

But underneath, feeling it's a waste

Let it out, I should, I would, I could

6. THE OLD ME

Sometimes I feel good

Sometimes I'm plain numb

Cause time has showed me

It waits for no-one

And now I miss the old me

I miss being innocent

I miss I'd do chores

And then make a few cents

I miss being ignorant

I know it makes no sense

But the more I think about things

The more it hurts staying on the fence

Dividing me up internally

Stuck living in the past

Or stressing about the future

Just wasting away

All my todays

Reminiscing and stressing

And then counting days

I'm starting to relate to the darkest songs

It's cool that I can,

but I wish that I didn't

I wish I could even for a moment

Feel a glimpse of the old me

7.   HOW FAR I'VE COME

Look,

I'm not where I want to be yet

But glad I'm not where I used to be

Sometimes when I sit back and reflect

I ask what the old me would think

Although I can barely remember

The thoughts I had back in November

I've moved on from that dark stage

I'm taking on the challenges coming of age

I've been dreading that moment,

But it might be time to be turning the page

The old me is but memories

The current me will make history

So the future me may look back with glory

And reflect on how far I had come

8.   WORDS I WROTE

"There's a knife in my room, somebody put it there"

Those were the words I wrote

When I was mentally still there

Only then, would I truly know

What those words really meant to me

When suicidal thoughts came up constantly

Hoping they'd just leave already,

But they kept going at it so damn relentlessly

9.   EMPTY

Lately,

Every thing feels, empty

If only I could wake up

From this, bad dream

If only I had it all

Planned out, nicely

Maybe then I would

Stop tossing around

In, my sleep

Lately,

I've been feeling, empty

If only I would get up

Go chase, that dream

If only I knew it'd all

Work out, nicely

Maybe then I could

Have sweet dreams inbound

And, might sleep

10. THE GOOD OLD DAYS

I miss the days when I was innocent

And won the award for being an optimist

All I am today is just an agonist

Living every day like a clone of yesterday

The minute goes so slow yet the hours fly so fast

Spending present days looking back at my old past

Jealous of myself when life was such a blast

Better days are far away, the shadows that they cast

Only amplifies the pain, searching for it, standing on the mast

11. MAYBE (I)

What does it mean to be happy?

What if it's something I can't be?

Maybe I just need therapy

Losing myself in poetry

Told myself, grow up, get a life and you'll see

So satisfied with life, I thought I'd be

Honestly wish I were still that naive

Take my issues and bury 'em six feet

I don't wanna deal with them now, just leave me alone

Procrastinate cause I don't know how, I'm all on my own

Maybe that's the way that I like it

Maybe that's what I'd have wanted

Maybe, oh maybe just maybe I'm just trying to stop feeling jaded

12. MAYBE (II)

You know, sometimes I sit down and ask myself what I'm even doing.

Like what's even the point of doing any of this and I really can't give myself a good answer.

Maybe I just can't.

It's like I'm living life to just try and escape it.

It's like I'm running after it but don't why I chase it

Would be nice if I knew what it is that I am chasing

Maybe then, I could get rid of all of the faking

Growing up, I dreamed that I would make it

What if I did, but turns out that I hate it

What if I made it to the end of my life

And watched all of my memories unwind

And then realized I wasn't even alive

I'd feel like I'd be losing my mind

Finally finding that knot that's inside

Finally taking it out and see it unwind

All these years, it's been tossed helplessly aside

Maybe if I really opened my eyes

And had the vision to see through the lies

Then I'd finally realize, I ain't afraid of my demise

13.   18 YEARS OLD

I'm writing this at sixteen

The future to me still seems

Like a movie I haven't yet seen

Reminiscing 'bout my dreams

The future kinda scares me

Thinking 'bout it got me weary

I wonder what I'll be like I'm eighteen

Will I even be me

Will the future still be scary

Or will I find something-

That will finally make me

Be able to feel what it's like to be happy

Talk about the past like it's history

Feels like yesterday I was in my seat

On the back of the school bus, My mind full of fantasy

I was so innocent then, I would make myself believe

Things would get better, there's no need to worry.

Nowadays I don't even know

What I'll have in store for my future self to show

Nothing much, except nostalgia aglow

Will I take my chances, or just let it blow

Will I keep my stances, on everything I know

Under these circumstances, how could I say no

The answer to that, I truly do not know

When I'm eighteen, guess I'll see how much I've grown

Will I be excited getting out of bed

Or would I lay there wishing to be dead

Will I be proud of what I did

Or would my heart be weak as lead

24

14. A YEAR AGO

25

I remember it like it yesterday

I was sitting in this very room, my hair done right and headphones on the side

I remember so vividly, it was my first time

Sleeping overnight in this new room,

Joining a Hackathon real soon

Everything'd gone virtual but that's alright

I still took every opportunity to reach new heights

I talked with my friend from elementary school

Who I'd volunteered with at the swimming pool

Got my feels already, man those days were cool

I take one pause,

One blink of the eye

And before I- knew it,

I had grown all too soon

A year ago, still fresh in my mind

Like tracks in freshly laid snow

There's just nothing like it, one of a kind

As I always say,

The days we count pass so slowly

But the months lost count so quickly

And before I knew it, I'm in a different year completely

I remember when I were young, time would pass so slow

A single year worth a fifth of my life on this planet

I dread the day when a year feels like it was nothing

And watch as my energy and days start waning

But that's too far into the future, right

Those exact words I spoke about where I am today

That feeling in life that just never goes away

Spending the present thinking about the past

Or thinking about the future

I guess a year ago,

I never thought this year would go

By so fast but so slow

Slow in the moment,

But if every moment's the same,

The days, they merge together inside the brain

15. PERFECTIONIST

You could say I'm a little bit messed up

Obsessing over details you'll never see the end of

Perfecting every line and

every rhyme and every time

I mess up a syllable

It feels a bit criminal

It seems almost comical

How much thought I put into

Overthinking things I really

Shouldn't be thinking that hard about

And it keeps on bothering me that

I can't seem to keep these thoughts out

I've got a poster on my wall telling me

Done is better than perfect, ironically-

I still keep on overthinking when-

I could have finished but then-

I make it take longer by a magnitude of ten-

I keep it going, how long can-

I keep it flowing, it's just that-

I don't know when it's time-

I should have stop even if-

I know it but still can't feel it-

I am finally deciding that-

I had enough and I'm finally stopping.

It's not just not being able to finish what I

Wanted to get done that bother me,

But also the fact that it's fostering

My destructive habit of procrastinating

See, it seems like it's even more difficult

For me to get started than it's difficult

For me to finish what I'd already started

16.   TAKE OFF

Passing time, yeah

Feels like I'm just passing time

Feels like I ain't living right

They ask me what I'm doing,

I'm just passing time

Yeah, I'm escaping life

I've got a lotta things but

I don't have a life yeah

I just need a life

I just need some time

I need to meditate

Happiness from within,

No need to medicate

Feels like everything they gave to me

Is so over rate - ed

If I saw what life had in store for me

Prolly woulda fainted

Yeah, I wish I could just change it

You know I'm gonna change it

Sick of all the same stuff

I'm the one to make it

Miss me with that fake bit

Climb up to the top and then

Look down like what's poppin?

Wanna catch up to me,

You gon' need a rocket

I'll be in the cockpit

I'm about to drive this ship so far out, damn

Hyperdrive mode, it's out beyond the stars, man

No need to worry, trip's on me, fam

Light it quickly, trips on lean and

Wakes up later to find out it was all a dream, dang

I find it kinda funny

How you really did believe

I'd take you with me on this trip

When you've done nothing but make me trip

You the type to call my stuff pretty lit

And then behind my back, call it stupid

Fell for it already, or did I?

Fall for it again, how could I?

Look into my eyes, I won't lie

17. THE ROLLER COASTER I DIDN'T ASK TO BE ON

Roller Coasters, I've never really liked them

Not that I was scared or had something against them

but I didn't see the point in waiting

And baking under the scorching sun

For what felt like an eternity

Just to get into a cart and climb slowly

Up a steep and exhausting hill,

Not being able to see over it,

Or what lay on the other side of it,

But pursuing something regardless

Squinting to see under the glaring sunlight

Wondering if it would ever stop

Or if I would ever know why I got on

Talking to the others on this Discombobulator,

Everybody in their own seats,

Some on the sides with a different view from others

But nobody knowing how long we had left to go

The conversations all around me

And the friends that all surround me,

At that moment, I knew I'd finally found it,

This was the very reason why I boarded this coaster

The cranking of gears and chains signaled the end,

The end of this long haul as the train momentarily stopped

With the sun hidden behind a huge veil of now glowing clouds,

We could finally see the world from its top

The city's skyline decorated the horizon with colossal skyscrapers

The breathtaking view from above, revealed to us everything

We had come all this way up for this and we savored that feeling

At that moment, I knew I'd finally found it,

This was the very reason why I boarded this coaster

But like anything else, nothing good stays that way forever

As the coaster started moving again, the front started tipping

Soon, the back followed and the pace quickened

Before we knew it, we were plummeting down

Down towards the very ground we rose up from

The howling wind blowing our hair back,

Going into our eyes and making it hard to see again

But though we were plummeting down

And losing all we had worked for on the journey up,

There was a foreign yet pleasurable sensation

It was thrilling, but relaxing, and without a hesitation,

We threw our hands into the air, feeling the wind weave its way

Through our fingers as we hollered and laughed

This was the reward of everything,

The wait, the climb and grind up to the top,

All that just to lead to this very moment

And at that moment, I knew I'd finally found it,

This was the very reason why I boarded this coaster

18. BITTERSWEET TREE SAP

You meant the world to me

You meant so much to me

You were that light at the

end of this treacherous tunnel

You were my reason why

I ever even bothered to try

You've made me who I am

You've built me from the sand

You were there when I needed a hand

You were there when life tasted so bland-

And you mixed it up and made it so sweet

I know not how you did, for it was no easy feat

You cheered me on amidst my victory

You cheered me up amidst my defeat

You are the one that always remembered me

You were the one that gave me your seat

You put me into this world, the rest is history

Said that little shrub you nurtured so gracefully

But that shrub, it grew up so hastefully

The soil so abundant in nutrients,

The sun shining strong, but not blazingly

That shrub soon outgrew the planters, with all the ingredients

You provided it so generously

This shrub's roots are getting longer,

The pot it sits in helps it no longer

The pot cracks from the root's pressure

It opens up and the roots reach out below

Into the soil, finding a place of its own

Roots expanding into the earth, searching for home

It gets cold on some days, chilled to the bone

But heed with caution for

Though with good intention, your

Warmth is merely temporary

And some days, it's better off cold and frozen

For the sap inside still remains ambrosian

And that sap reaps, forever bitter sweet

19. MODERN SOCIETY

Yeah I'm feeling kinda numb today

It's that feeling again that just won't go away

If you had a choice, would you leave or choose to stay

I don't really know, but I don't wanna live this way

It just goes to show that we're livin' on stage

It's just funny how they talk to behinds, but not to their face

Everybody stressed about what others think of them lately

I'm just watching this, man this world is goin' crazy

They really do be trying to blind me

What's it? Bigot, fool or slave?

I really couldn't tell ya, blimey

I'm the one trying to save

The people the keyboard warriors gonna slay

In the end, it's us all that have to pay

It does good for no-one, I just gotta say

If they ain't gonna listen, all I've got is to pray

To the lord that everything's gonna be okay

If I stay out of it and act like I'm doing it their way

I thought about it, looked up and said to him, no wait

What's the point in knowing the truth if

I don't do anything and it bothers me

Knowing that people are going around

And saying they fighting for equality

But knowing that they're doing it selectively

As if their actions were done almost maliciously

Are these external sources brainwashing me

Or are they simply just making me see clearly

See, it's hard to decide who to believe

With all these narratives going around,

I've chosen my side carefully

It's sad to see though,

On both sides are friends and enemies

Just push through it, head up and ears close maybe

I'll be going through it solo probably

I think it's better off that way, but I guess we'll see

I'll do what it takes and I

Will thrive in this modern society

20. NOW THAT YOU'RE GONE

Now that you're gone, I'll try to go on

But it's hard to move on

When you're stuck in that zone

Breaking my bones, but cleaning my soul

Wish it were us, but I'll do it alone

Please don't make me leave what I'd known

It'll be hard, but I need you out of my phone

The constant reminders keep chilling my bone

Perhaps you'll be at peace with a gravestone

Reminiscing about all the things that we've done

I want the real you, not just some clone